VAGUE

Interview with Arnold Schwarzenegger not in this issue. Sorry—Arnold was originally to be standing beside this vehicle in full camouflage army fatigues but could not be found. We rented the Hummer, we rented the field, Arnold didn't show.

fashion

health & beauty

features

ABOVE:
Karl Lagerhead's
New Minimalism
look is taking off.

RIGHT:
Karl Lagerhead
has his finger on the
pulse of the fashion
world.

OTHER BOOKS FROM THE SAME TWISTED MIND

AUTOGRAPHED COPIES BY MAIL ORDER

To purchase a personally autographed copy of *Vague, Cowsmopolitan, Playboar* or *Penthorse*, send $13 US (money order or bank draft) plus $4 shipping and handling per book (outside North America, $7 shipping and handling per book) to:

Books
Box 32001
Cambridge, Ontario
Canada N3H 5M2

or order through our website at:
www.vagueworld.com

YOUR LIFE STORY IN SHOCKING BOLD PRINT!

Send the author your most interesting stories of embarrassment, humiliation, humor, shopping, PMS, dating or fashion. They could end up in his next book. E-mail:

thagey@vagueworld.com (« click here now all web surfers… it won't help but it can't hurt).

VAGUE

A FIREFLY BOOK

Cataloguing in Publication Data
Hagey, Thomas
Vague
ISBN 1-55209-056-6
1. Fashion - Humor. 2. Beauty, Personal - Humor.
3. Vogue - Parodies, imitations, etc. I. Title.

PN6231.F36H33 1997   C818'.5402   C97-930858-5

VAGUE, written by Thomas Hagey, is not licensed by or affiliated in any way with any existing magazine or publication. It is strictly a parody.

Published in Canada by
Firefly Books Ltd.
3680 Victoria Park Avenue
Willowdale, Ontario
Canada M2H 3K1

Published in the U.S. by
Firefly Books (U.S.) Inc.
P.O. Box 1338, Ellicott Station
Buffalo, New York, 14205

Printed and bound in Canada

For Marlene De Boer
whose love, support,
and humor
made all of this
possible.

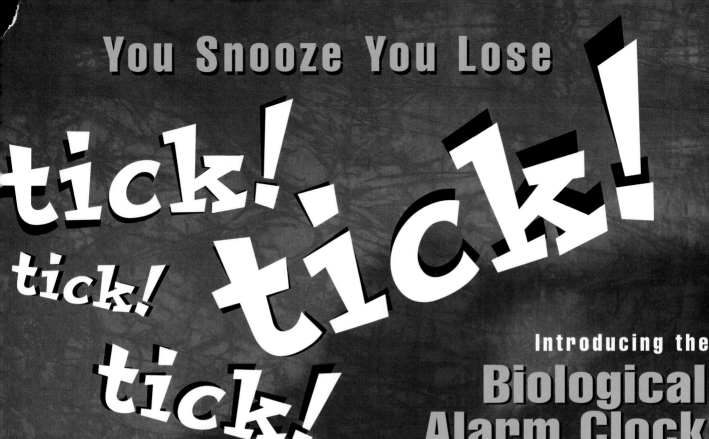

You Snooze You Lose

tick! tick! tick! tick! tick!

Introducing the
Biological Alarm Clock
from Panic-A-Sonic®

If you think that time is flying by—it is. And, if you're one of those women who don't want to wake up one day and say, **"Oh my God, I forgot to have children!"** then the Biological Alarm Clock Radio from Panic-A-Sonic® is one bedroom companion worth taking home. Avoid unnecessary last minute freakouts, with the daily biological wake up call from Panic-A-Sonic®.

One more good reason to wake up and smell the coffee

Panic-A-Sonic

11:59

FM 88 92 96 100 104 108 MHz
AM 53 60 70 80 100 130 170 mkHz

NEW from Panic-A-Sonic®

VAGUE

Created, Written and Produced by
Thomas Hagey

Art Direction & Design
Bob Wilcox

Fashion Photography: **Stan Switalski**, Cambridge, Canada
Product Photography: **Steve Lawrence**, Toronto
Creative Consultant/Editor: **Duncan McKenzie**
Copy Editing: **Dan Liebman**; **Angela Pollak**
Fashion Design: **Susan Dicks**, Toronto; **Brad Balch**, Kitchener, Canada
Photo Shoot Coordination **Stephanie Haynes**; **Abby King**
Art & Illustration: **David Prothero**; **Bruce Herchenrader**; **Michael Caunter**
Sean Dawdy; **Ted Sivell**; **Timm Vera**; **Chris Zakrzewski**
Props: **Boardwalk Optical**; **Rapp Optical**; **John Weber**; **Cambridge Towel**;
Brad Balch, the amazing prop maker; **James Sauder**; **Voll motors**
Production Assistance: **Jim Robinson**, Ignition Design; **TTS promotional apparel**, screen printing;
Ken Hartley, photo retouching; **Kevin Weight**, photo manipulation; **Kelvin Case**, North by Northwest;
Mark Bugdale, The Impact Group; **Susan Schaefer**; **Brian Wiebe**
Hair & Makeup: **Andrea Claire Walmsley**; **Heather Brooks**; **Collin Woods**; **Bilal Zeineddine**;
Laura Szucs; **Eve Hrubik**; **Irene Rockwell**; **Lisa Dennison**; **Kendra Schumacher**; **Tex Lillepool**;
Laurie Weichel; **Icon salon & spa**
Models & Actors: **Tara Sinnett**, cover model; **Mark Bergen**; **Marlene De Boer**; **Rob Nickerson**;
Naomi Blicker; **Jennifer Jacobson**; **Jennifer Faulds**; **Bruce Hunter**; **Katherine Ashby**;
Stephanie Haynes; **Janet Van De Graaff**; **Blair Bender**; **Teresa Pavlinek**; **Stephanie Guest**;
Jude Winterbottom; **Tammy Withrow**; **Lisa Maslanka**; **Jeff Maslanka**; **Heather Eve McKearnan**;
Michael Rouse; **Jennifer Swann**; **Collin Woods**; **Amanda Moir**; **Steven Wong**; **James Hall**;
Richard Sanders (AKA Les Nessman); **Vanessa Tikkala**; **Ross Fraser**; **Lora Zulijani**; **Sage Walmsley**;
Woodruff the Jack Russell by **Hot Pursuit Kennels**; Breeding pigs by the **Crow family**;
Melissa Wanklin; **Belise Abwunza**; **Sarah Cressman**; **Val Kinzie**
Special Thanks: **Richard Sanders**; **Hank Sternberg**; **Reid Bannister**; **Mary E. Lea**; **Donald Lea**;
The Beirnes family; **Kim & Paul McAuley**; **Alex & Vicky Taylor**; **Jim & Ellyn Robinson**;
Martin Meissner; **Abby King**; **Stankiewicz family**; **Lloyd & Bertha Hagey**; **Zwart family**;
Lakeroad Catering; **Media Focus**; **Dan Grady**; **Mark & Phyllis Silverstein** @ Studio City Guest
House and Spa; **Mike Melnychuk**; **Ted Giesbrecht**; **Jono Turlej**; **Kent & Cha Heiden**; **Pamela Main**;
Stanley Peter Owens; **Doug Scheerer**; **Tracey Alexander**; **Bruce Ettinger**; **Smith Hart** and everyone at
ICW; **Donald & Nancy Tikkala**; **Helene Couture**; **Janet Verrips**; **Deanna & Carl Gmelin**;
Circo Bar & Grill; **Gord & Judy Rottar**; **Randy Rodriguez, Rio Bravo Trading Company**, Santa Fe;
Harry Mathews; **John Whitney**; **Christina & Dave Tomlinson**; **Simpson Lumber**; **John Brunton**;
John Hagey; the **Beckers**; **Wendy Davis**; **Bob & Anke**; **Fernanda Sousa**; **Renée LaLonde**;
Amy McKenzie; **Lionel Koffler**; **Michael Worek**; **Superior Safety**; jet pilots, **Bill Robinson &
Stu Swanson**; **Fliteline Services Ground Crew**; **Bloomingdale Service**; **Dr. & Ms Achtymichuk**
Translation: **Vanessa Stankiewicz**; **Anke Davids**; **Nikka Times**; **Robert J. Ellis**; **Ke Xiang**; **Sean Song**

Stop Me Before I Scratch Again!

CURES MOST VAGINAL YEAST INFECTIONS TO A POINT

Femizoid-13™

13% CLOTRIMAZOLY-HOLY-SCHMOLY VAGINAL CREAM

SHOCKING EDUCATIONAL PAMPLETS INSIDE
©1997 Chema-ceuticals. For a brighter future – CHEMICALLY!!

ANTIFUNGAL
(13 HOUR
THERAPY)

If scratching isn't your idea of a balanced workout, then you may need the full-strength reliability of Femizoid 13.

Next yeast infection, try the simple cure: one oral tablet taken orally, and that's it— no more worries about *down there*.

Depend on Femizoid 13 for fast relief and a cure guaranteed in 13 hours or less, or we refund your money *and* pay for the manicure.

Femizoid 13 ®

...because sometimes life is itchy and unfair.

people are raving about

theater

ANDREW LLOYD WEBBER STUBS HIS BIG PHAT TOE

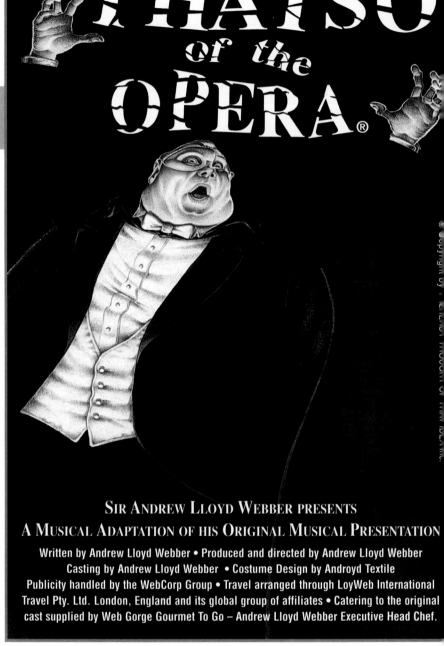

SIR ANDREW LLOYD WEBBER PRESENTS
A MUSICAL ADAPTATION OF HIS ORIGINAL MUSICAL PRESENTATION

Written by Andrew Lloyd Webber • Produced and directed by Andrew Lloyd Webber
Casting by Andrew Lloyd Webber • Costume Design by Androyd Textile
Publicity handled by the WebCorp Group • Travel arranged through LoyWeb International
Travel Pty. Ltd. London, England and its global group of affiliates • Catering to the original
cast supplied by Web Gorge Gourmet To Go – Andrew Lloyd Webber Executive Head Chef.

The opening of *Phatso Of The Opera* in London, England, has been tagged as Andrew Lloyd Webber's leap into the icy waters of political incorrectness. There was no shortage of drama as a packed house of loyal followers, dignitaries and media bigwigs witnessed the royal embarrassment. Lloyd Webber's condition is extremely unstable but not life threatening. He has been taken off the critical list and is reported to be recovering in hospital after a severely bruised ego caused him to collapse into the horn section of the orchestra, accidentally killing a musician. The trumpet player, whose name has not been released, died instantly when Lloyd Webber's enormous but delicate ego struck him on the temple.

The incident has left his fans numbed, his critics smacking their lips, and friends as well as hangers-on asking: "Andrew Lloyd Who?"

Lloyd Webber was never one to follow the crowd. But his decision to produce *Phatso* has cast a mammoth hulk of a shadow on his past success and places his entire future in jeopardy.

He could have named it *The Masked Rotundly Challenged Chap of the Opera,* but he chose not to. That would be too safe. As a result, on opening night, Fate's black chauffeur driven limousine quietly idled in the alleyway out back of the theater, patiently awaiting the rising of the curtain and the arrival of the next casualty. Fate, it seems, has all the time in the world. Ironically, the musical began with a fat lady singing. Need I say more? A short while later, much to Sir Andrew Lloyd's dislike, people began walking out of the show. In fact, it became so unpopular, people bought tickets just so they could walk out on it.

We're all tired of political correctness, but do we all go out and make a huge stage production out of it and jam it down the theater-going public's throats? No... (pause), we do not!

Was he hoping to fail? Is he tired of the Midas touch? Was *Phatso* self-sabotage? If not, why would a man of his class take such a creative risk at this point in his career?

Unfortunately we won't have any answers until they take the tubes out of his nose, and while they're at it, his big feet out of his mouth. VAGUE can only assume that Lloyd Webber had tired of political correctness and decided to say it like it is. A big mistake. Everyone hated it, with the exception of the Japanese media. They hailed it as charming, a huge success and a work of genius, but one should expect this brand of optimism from the nation which brought the world Sumo Wrestling.

The public has a difficult enough time dealing with the issue of fat without making matters worse. What possessed him to take such a delicate subject and set it to music? We may never know the answer.

Plans to launch two more politically incorrect productions based on other Andrew Lloyd Webber creations have been halted, at least for now. *Fat Cats* and *Sunset Bowl O'Lard* are temporarily in limbo until options regarding their marketing can be assessed. Judging by the public outrage aimed at *Phatso of the Opera* I would hazard a guess there is an Operatic Fat Lady somewhere at this very moment practicing her scales, waiting for opening night.

etter from the editor

W hile the world sleeps, we are applying the finishing touches to another issue of *VAGUE*. It has been a month of fashion moments.

Yves St. La Croix sends us another one of his scanty lingerie items hot off the plane from Paris. Five of our body perfect editors fight tooth and nail to be the first to try it on. The blood-soaked winner parades about our offices announcing in a monotone voice: "I'm the most beautiful woman in the world, and *this* is my story!"

Armando Armani (loose translation: "Your money or your life") also sends us his absolute best. There's no outfit... no large box of lingerie... no warning... just a postage-due "Greetings from Milan" postcard with a spontaneous doodle on the back. So perfect. So well chosen. So... *Armani!* We can only wonder how he finds the time to design amid his hectic letter-writing agenda.

The flurry of activity here at *VAGUE* can only mean one thing: "Once again" fashion is on the move. "Once again" designers are emerging from gout treatment clinics; "once again" they have sworn off anything in a heavy cream sauce. But why? When are these male designers going to realize that "tossing your cookies" is no longer reserved for those gloriously trim, emaciated models. It was good enough for Roman centurions; it's surely good enough for overweight designers.

But enough about the industry's jagged little pill. Let's retire gorge and purge to the back burner and get on with the business of fashion. It's a challenge to reinvent the wheel season after season. If you intend to stay on top you can't rest on your laurels or you risk becoming "a fat ass." "Once again" the designers are promising to deliver quality and originality at a price which will allow them to cover their overheads comfortably.

TOP RIGHT: JEAN CLAUDE CLOD'S NOW-FAMOUS LETTUCE HAT

BOTTOM LEFT: CEO/DESIGNER HARRY KRISHNA IS THE NEW CAT'S ASS OF THE FASHION WORLD

RIGHT: SOME WOMAN WHO WANDERED INTO MY OFFICE ONE DAY CLAIMING TO BE A MAN TRAPPED IN A WOMAN'S CLOTHES

With the recession now officially over, it is "once again" okay to appear rich. Frugality is still in, but now it's expensive. "Once again" we encourage you to cough up the big bucks; it's what separates the Lady of the house from the hired help.

This month **Umberto Garbaggio** reinvents the bag lady with his recycled fabrics collection, **Krishna Dior** continues his climb to prominence as his divine fashion consciousness catches fire, and **Jean Claude Clod** redefines *Hat Couture,* proving "once again" that it's not what's inside your head that counts.

All things considered, it should be an exciting issue. At this point we ask that you sit back, relax, enjoy the trip; we should be landing in Paris shortly. Have a great day and remember that although there's nothing wrong with looking fabulous, fashion *has* been described as the subtle art of self-deception. Self-deception: the ingenious ability of pulling the wool over your own eyes.

Anna Whirlwintour

Vague trends

by contributing writer
Lance Boyle

The Zit is a Hit!

THE SIMPLE PIMPLE SQUEEZES ITS WAY INTO THE LIMELIGHT

Over the centuries the mole has been admired as a symbol of beauty. Some of the most idolized women in the world have had moles: Marilyn Monroe, Elizabeth Taylor, Madonna and Cindy Crawford. What was it that launched these glamorous careers? A great body? Talent? Or a brown blemish with the hair in the middle?

Yes, it was the mole which twisted the rubbery arm of popularity in their favor.

For years the mole has been the blot of beauty, the queen of the molehill, numero uno. But is it on the verge of being replaced? Now a new contender threatens to burrow away at the mole's sex appeal and alluring grip on the fashion-conscious public. We refer, of course, to the pimple.

In this issue of *VAGUE* we take a look behind the zit phenomenon that has taken the world by storm. We learn to say Au revoir MOLE and Bonjour ZIT.

The Unusual Becomes Beautiful

It may have taken the world by surprise, but there is nothing unusual about the zit's popularity and rapid rise to prominence. Like POISON perfume before it, the negative image surrounding the zit has done nothing to limit its appeal. Quite the opposite—the threat, the daring stigma, the taboo of the zit is an essential part of its fascination. Starting out as a barely noticeable blip on the lip of fashion this pustule outcast has grown and risen, until its popularity has reached the point of exploding.

A New "Pop" Icon—
What's the Fuss About Pus?

The arrival of the pimple on the world stage has left beauty experts miffed, cosmetic and chemaceutical company executives worried and supermodels scrambling to grow their own, get bacterial implants or pack their clothes and go home.

Could anyone have foreseen such a turnabout? A few short months ago it was every young woman's nightmare. A condition which added more anxiety to the pre-prom night jitters than the anticipation of losing one's virginity to some fumbling, insensitive, adolescent guy. Yet the zit has become all the rage. No matter where you go—clubs, cafés, the opera—the zit is not only on everyone's lips but on their chins, foreheads and cheeks as well.

No longer is the zit youth's fashion statement. Its popularity bulges through barriers of age, race and financial status. Beauty watchers claim you can tell a person's true wealth by the way they carry their zits. People of "old money" display them discreetly around the neckline or beside the ear, one more thing comfortably within their grasp. Whereas the nouveau riche tend to flaunt their newfound wealth by squeezing them in public.

The Zit Is Here To Stay

Like false eyelashes and fake fingernails, it looks like the zit will be around for quite some time. If you're squeamish brace yourself. You will wear one eventually. You will stand in line with everyone else to get that doozy of an oozy.

Battle Against Zit Comes To Head

Not everyone is embracing the trend. The manufacturers of acne-fighting formulas have watched in horror as profits plunged to all-time lows. Says one executive, "We're literally getting squeezed out of the market." Many of these companies have collectively injected advertising dollars toward a media blitz to convince the public that the trend is goofy and potentially dangerous. The campaign is not considered a lost gauze as yet, but early indications reveal they aren't soaking up much support with it either.

Juicy Profits In Zit Accessories

Zitco, manufacturers of *The Zit Kit*, and their competition *Acme Acne Inc.*, makers of *Squeeze Me, I'm Yours,* are the first two companies out on the market with implants and stick-ons. Both have reported landslide profits and are extremely optimistic about their future in fostering festering, but neither has forgotten what happened to the now defunct Dow Corning Company, the breast implant giant that sought bankruptcy protection when their hooters came home to roost.

Still, so far (touch silicone) everyone is very pleased with their zit implants, but trends change. There are no guarantees to manufacturers that recipients won't sue. As long as the courts keep awarding huge settlements, legal battles will continue to flare up and run rampant.

The Zit Kit, manufactured by Zitco, is sweeping the globe. These stick-on accessories offer fashion-conscious consumers the instant zit look. ($59)

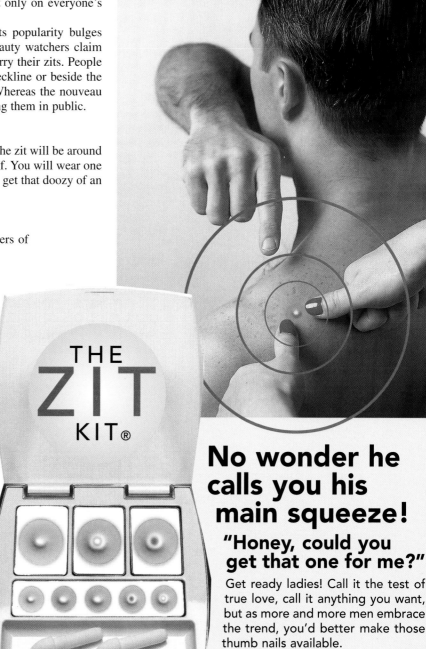

THE ZIT KIT®

No wonder he calls you his main squeeze!
"Honey, could you get that one for me?"

Get ready ladies! Call it the test of true love, call it anything you want, but as more and more men embrace the trend, you'd better make those thumb nails available.

Vague books

Sunny Rhodes breaks new ground in the "How To" book genre, with the landmark release of *The Merry Widow.* This step-by-step guide is a must-read for any woman who has patiently, patiently, run out of patience.

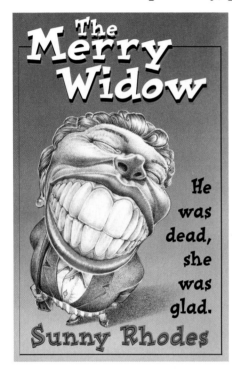

The Merry Widow: He was dead, she was glad.

By Sunny Rhodes

They say happiness doesn't happen by accident. The Merry Widow is the exception to the rule. Mr. Never-Been-Wrong isn't coming home for dinner anymore and somebody in the house is very glad.

This moving book is one woman's testimony on how to achieve happiness through accidental expiration. The struggle for independence, which leads her to a course in auto mechanics and brake line maintenance. A course from which she would eventually earn an "A" plus. An "A" plus which would lead to that lonely, slippery stretch of highway known as Devil's Bend. As for her husband, it's too bad Todd isn't here to join in the fun, but "them's the brakes!" Female determination and a great deal of insurance have paved the way to a much merrier future for the author.

$22.95 Hardcorpse, Graves & Jyvanaditch Publishers N.Y. N.Y.

Beyond The Fridge: Food For Thought

by Candice B. Wolfed

The diet book that takes you out of the kitchen, out of the house, onto the streets and into the exciting new world of possibilities.

Ahh! the beckoning fridge. Many a woman's battle with low self-esteem begins here. Take control of your life. Learn to resist the "Snack Attack."

Over 100 pages of Calorie-reduced advice and Fat-free alternatives which will ultimately lead to a happier you. This book demonstrates how to recognize the fine line between "Having A Wee Bite To Eat" and "Slamming The Groceries Into You!" It hammers home the message that although supermarkets have hundreds of items, they don't all have to end up back at your place. Remember, they have other customers too.

$24.95 Simon & Shister, The Self Help Specialists

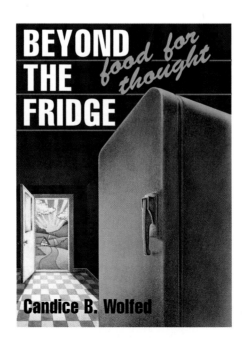

Cross Dogs And Over Anxious Women

by Lyle Lyttle

"There was a time when a woman never took her man to the cleaners unless his suit actually needed pressing."

At last! The riveting history of the feminist movement written from a man's perspective. A lightly spirited chronicling of the fight not only for equality, but for the unfair advantage women now enjoy in a world once dominated by men.

You will relive the helpless male years when men didn't vacuum, didn't babysit, didn't watch their backs during PMS—but simply stood there and took it like a man. You'll visit a time when men refused to cook or pick up the kids from day care, or bear their souls, or exercise their feminine side because they'd be called "wimp."

Yes, thanks to the movement many men are now champions and serious rivals in a world of worthy domestic chores once dominated by women. They are still, however, accused of being wimps, but they are secure in the knowledge that the feminist movement was partly about the liberation of men; and for this they have the stronger sex to thank—women, of course!

Hardcover $29.95 Rangdom House Publishers New York New York

MATURITY®

FOR MEN

AFTER

Calvin Kline
eau de toilette

MATURITY
FOR MEN

eau de toilette

Men and maturity?

Sounds like a
contradiction in terms...
until now.

MATURITY
from Calvin Kline

His Art Hangs in the White House But His Latest Work Has Been Created Just for You.

The Lady with the Ball and Chain

(also known as "Our Lady of Perpetual Crankiness") is now available in snow-white porcelain from who else but The Frankly Mint.

The art of Gianini Porcelini is in museums and priceless collections around the world. His newest masterpiece promises not only to enhance the elegance of your home but will alert members of the opposite sex that there is, indeed, a lady in the house. And for about a week out of every month, they may well be living on borrowed time. Tweaked your interest yet? There's more!

Inspired by the blue and white porcelain of Josiah Wedgwood over 200 years ago, this marble-like porcelain will be treasured for its depth, width, height and delicate detail. Not to mention the thrill of partial nakedness.

This enchanting cameo captures the legend of "That Special Time" (often, for good reasons, referred to as The Wrong Time) and achieves this like no other work of art. It is splendidly matted in linen and framed in solid realistic wood, ready to display.

Frankly, it's only available from The Frankly Mint. And quite frankly, if you don't place your order quickly, this limited edition will be sold out. This specially imported work is priced at only $295—very reasonable for handcrafted porcelain art by an internationally renowned artist, spotlighting a subject as delicate as this one. Frankly, we've never before seen quality of this caliber at such an affordable price.

His previous works pertaining to women's issues, most notably *Guilt* & *Laundry,* sold out in less than a month. Don't be disappointed. Reserve NOW!!!

The Lady with the Ball and Chain

The burden of menstruation
NOW IN SNOW-WHITE PORCELAIN

The Frankly Mint... *We put stuff in your house.*®

© Frankly Mint

Vague movies

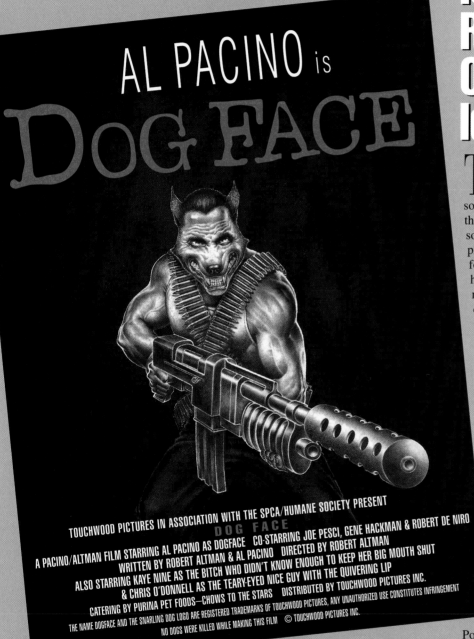

AL PACINO is

DOG FACE

TOUCHWOOD PICTURES IN ASSOCIATION WITH THE SPCA/HUMANE SOCIETY PRESENT
DOG FACE
A PACINO/ALTMAN FILM STARRING AL PACINO AS DOGFACE   CO-STARRING JOE PESCI, GENE HACKMAN & ROBERT DE NIRO
WRITTEN BY ROBERT ALTMAN & AL PACINO   DIRECTED BY ROBERT ALTMAN
ALSO STARRING KAYE NINE AS THE BITCH WHO DIDN'T KNOW ENOUGH TO KEEP HER BIG MOUTH SHUT
& CHRIS O'DONNELL AS THE TEARY-EYED NICE GUY WITH THE QUIVERING LIP
CATERING BY PURINA PET FOODS—CHOWS TO THE STARS   DISTRIBUTED BY TOUCHWOOD PICTURES INC.
THE NAME DOGFACE AND THE SNARLING DOG LOGO ARE REGISTERED TRADEMARKS OF TOUCHWOOD PICTURES. ANY UNAUTHORIZED USE CONSTITUTES INFRINGEMENT
NO DOGS WERE KILLED WHILE MAKING THIS FILM   © TOUCHWOOD PICTURES INC.

Is Hollywood Running Out Of Original Ideas?

The public is being served up remakes, something-likes, sequels and rehashes to the point of nausea. Not only do the titles sound identical but the story lines are suspiciously familiar as well. It's a formula for success which doesn't necessarily have anything to do with great entertainment—and an illness that you shouldn't expect to disappear just yet.

Dog Face, the latest release from Touch Wood Pictures Inc, starring Al Pacino, does not fall into the retread, tediously thin on substance category. This vaguely familiar cross between two of Pacino's earlier hits, *Scarface* and *Dog Day Afternoon,* is both powerful and riveting. American movie critics Sisko & Egbert loved it so much they gave it the first-ever *four thumbs up* rating.

Pacino works his magic as Dog Face. There's biting suspense, and the action never stops.

Touch Wood Pictures keeps walking the tightrope as rumors of another Pacino-cast canine theme film is currently in development. *Scent of a Dog* is to commence shooting next June, followed next spring by *Dogfather—Life's a Bitch in the Mafia...* Are they longshots? Possibly, but if anyone can pull it off it'll be Al Pacino.

Dog Face
Touch Wood Pictures Inc.
Al Pacino is back and he's off to South America to kick the drug lords' asses. Only this time he has a bit of a supernatural surprise in store for them. Killer suspense leaves the audience howling, snarling and begging for more.

"Pacino is powerful, riveting, larger than life! We haven't seen such a thriller since the release of **Bad Girl's Dormitory**. Non-stop crescendo of action, suspense and Milk-Boners—**A big Four Thumbs Up**"
–Sisko & Egbert, movie critics to the world

MORE
Vague movies

Waterworld II– The Last Bath

It floated into the theaters this month but failed to take the public by storm. It's the non-awaited sequel to Waterworld. Judging by the box office receipts, the only people who were really impatiently awaiting it were the investors of Waterworld I. They already paid for the horrendously expensive set and the axed action footage from the original movie, so why not attempt to retrieve some of that $200 million budget?

Sisko & Egbert Introduce Four Thumbs Up Rating

HOLLYWOOD – When somebody talks about putting four thumbs up, I immediately ask where? and whose? I fear with all these loose references to thumbs that the word *swiveling* is not too far away, and I don't like it one little bit.

Recently Sisko & Egbert—movie critics to the world—released news of their Four Thumbs Up film rating. Hopefully it means that Hollywood will be delivering more for the moviegoer's dollar. Don't hold your breath. It won't be long before the public discovers that four thumbs up is really just two thumbs up with two extra thumbs thrown in to keep pace with inflation.

KEVIN COSTNER
WATERWORLD II
THE LAST BATH

UNIVERSAL PICTURES AND WISH UPON A STAR ENTERTAINMENT CONSORTIUM PRESENT
WATERWORLD II – THE LAST BATH
STARRING KEVIN (JUST READ THE CONTRACT!) COSTNER   ALSO STARRING DENNIS HOPPER AS THE MAN WHO WOULDN'T DIE
MUSIC BY: OBVIOUSLY SOMEONE KEVIN PICKED   DIRECTED INDIRECTLY BY KEVIN COSTNER/GUN TO THEIR HEADS PRODUCTIONS
SOUND BY DOLBY   MR. COSTNER'S PADDLE BOAT BY BUD'S BUDGET AQUATIC VEHICLES
WHISKEY BY JACK DANIELS   CIGARETTES COMPLIMENTS OF R.J. REYNOLDS
DISTRIBUTED TO SOME EXTENT BY UNIVERSAL PICTURES INC. © UNIVERSAL PICTURES INC.

"Gone is the recycled urine-drinking scene in the first minute of the film. Aside from that, it's the same old same old..."

Waterworld II – The Last Bath
Universal Pictures

Gone is the recycled urine-drinking scene in the first minute of the film. Dennis Hopper makes an amazing return from hell... And Kevin Costner is definitely one strange kinda guy. Why would a young and virile male—for the second time— choose drifting around on a boat in an ocean of indifference when he has a chance to live out a fantasy with a beautiful woman on an island with an endless supply of Jack Daniels whiskey?... It may take one more sequel for the investors to get their money back.

For Work Or Foreplay

Rebellious Foreplay-Proof!® LipColors

We've employed a lot of dummies to perfect our latest LipColors.

New rebellious Foreplay-Proof® lipsticks from Revelon... They won't kiss off no matter how many dummies you encounter.

Vague movies
THE SEQUELS CONTINUE

So just how does Hollywood come up with all those boffo movie titles, anyway? With idea reserves running increasingly low, many are using computers to generate new titles automatically from existing titles. Check out where the industry is heading with some of these possible remakes and future smash hit sequels!

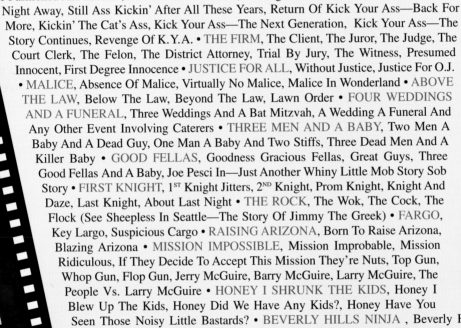

DIE HARD, Die Harder, Do or Die Even Harder, Die Hardest, Live And Let Die Hard • SLEEPING WITH THE ENEMY, Sleeping Through An Enema, Sleeping With The Nanny • SLEEPLESS IN SEATTLE, Sleeveless In Seattle, Sheepless In Seattle—The Story Of Jimmy The Greek • JEAN-CLAUDE VANN DAMME In: Kick Your Ass 1, Kick Your Ass 2, Kick My Ass Or I'll Kick Yours, Good Olde Fashioned Ass Kickin', Son Of Kick Your Ass, Waiting To Kick Your Ass, Ass Kickin' The Night Away, Still Ass Kickin' After All These Years, Return Of Kick Your Ass—Back For More, Kickin' The Cat's Ass, Kick Your Ass—The Next Generation, Kick Your Ass—The Story Continues, Revenge Of K.Y.A. • THE FIRM, The Client, The Juror, The Judge, The Court Clerk, The Felon, The District Attorney, Trial By Jury, The Witness, Presumed Innocent, First Degree Innocence • JUSTICE FOR ALL, Without Justice, Justice For O.J. • MALICE, Absence Of Malice, Virtually No Malice, Malice In Wonderland • ABOVE THE LAW, Below The Law, Beyond The Law, Lawn Order • FOUR WEDDINGS AND A FUNERAL, Three Weddings And A Bat Mitzvah, A Wedding A Funeral And Any Other Event Involving Caterers • THREE MEN AND A BABY, Two Men A Baby And A Dead Guy, One Man A Baby And Two Stiffs, Three Dead Men And A Killer Baby • GOOD FELLAS, Goodness Gracious Fellas, Great Guys, Three Good Fellas And A Baby, Joe Pesci In—Just Another Whiny Little Mob Story Sob Story • FIRST KNIGHT, 1ST Knight Jitters, 2ND Knight, Prom Knight, Knight And Daze, Last Knight, About Last Night • THE ROCK, The Wok, The Cock, The Flock (See Sheepless In Seattle—The Story Of Jimmy The Greek) • FARGO, Key Largo, Suspicious Cargo • RAISING ARIZONA, Born To Raise Arizona, Blazing Arizona • MISSION IMPOSSIBLE, Mission Improbable, Mission Ridiculous, If They Decide To Accept This Mission They're Nuts, Top Gun, Whop Gun, Flop Gun, Jerry McGuire, Barry McGuire, Larry McGuire, The People Vs. Larry McGuire • HONEY I SHRUNK THE KIDS, Honey I Blew Up The Kids, Honey Did We Have Any Kids?, Honey Have You Seen Those Noisy Little Bastards? • BEVERLY HILLS NINJA , Beverly Hills Cop 1, 2 & 3, Little Beverly Hills Snot • BRAD PITT in: Legends Of The Fall, The Legend Of Those Fools • SCARFACE, Cigar Face, Bizarre Face, Guitar Face • GUILTY BY SUSPICION, Beyond Suspicion, Above Suspicion, We're Not Suspicious And We Don't Give A Shit If He's Guilty Either • BOILING POINT, Vanishing Point, What's Your Point?, Don't Point! • PRIMAL RAGE, Primal Fear, Primal Instinct, Primal Horniness, Primal Time Television • STEVEN SEGAL in: Under Siege, Under Sarge—Steven Segal Meets Sgt. Bilko, On Dangerous Ground, On Bumpy Terrain, Hard To Kill • SCHINDLER'S LIST, Schindler's Other List, Schindler's Christmas Wish List, Schindler's Lips, Schindler's Lisp • JUST CAUSE, Just Because—And Don't Ask So Many Bloody Questions • MURDER BY DEATH, Murder For No Apparent Reason, Murder In The 1ST, 2ND & 3RD, Murder By Intercourse—The Trial Of Johnny The Schlong, Murder By Dangerous Indiscretion, Murder By Proxy, Murder Because Of Primal Rage With Extreme Prejudice And Without Just Cause • SENSE AND SENSIBILITY, Senseless But I Sense Stability, Incest And Sensitivity • FREE WILLY, Free Willy Too, Free Your Wet Willie, Free Willie Winkie, Either Lock It Up Or Let The Damn Fish Go Free—One Or The Other!!!

Does art imitate life? Or does mediocrity imitate success?

Shop Till You Drop!

Our Customers Come Last.

At American Excess, our customers come last. But, when it comes to shopping, any fool knows whoever finishes last wins.

You too can win big if you shop with the American Excess Platinum® card. It gets you what you want—even what you don't need—faster than any card we know of. And with no pre-set spending limit, your legs will give out before your credit does.

So, "shop till you drop" and experience the amazing difference that Platinum makes.

American Excess... membership has its casualties.®

Youthful skin is just the beginning.

Is your cleansing puff
trying to tell you something?

OIL
OLD of LADY

A breakthrough? You bet it is!

Scientists at OIL OF OLD LADY have made an exciting discovery. They've uncovered a rich oil in mature women which combats the aging process. We believe it achieves this in much the same way that the venom of poisonous snakes acts as an antidote for victims of snake bites. When used as directed, Oil Of Old Lady gently turns back the hands of time, producing results which stop at nothing short of remarkable. It's so effective in the prevention of lines and wrinkles that, by comparison, it makes Retin-A and Alpha Hydroxy Acids seem like… well, 'Snake Oil.' It actually reverses the process of aging, leaving your skin firm, smooth and supple—like no other product in the history of the world. All this in a shower scrub! And, when administered as intended, it not only eliminates odors, but delivers youthful-looking skin almost overnight.

Which brings us to the moral question...

We'd like to dismiss the rumors and innuendo flying around about kidnaping the elderly, missing persons and ritual grindings. In their selfish undying pursuit of fortune and publicity, it appears that our competitors will stop at nothing to maintain their own unfair share of the market. These allegations of unethical conduct are not only damaging and unfounded... they're really starting to annoy us. So, once and for all for the record, "We have done nothing WRONG!"

However, if you know of a loved one who would like to further the cause of scientific discovery, please don't hesitate to sign the donor card on the back of that special someone's driver's license. Then call this toll-free number for more information about our no-obligation money-making opportunity.

Phone: 1-800-SELL-GRANNY.
No detailed questions asked.
No further correspondence.
Offer void where prohibited
(but we're negotiating with politicians).

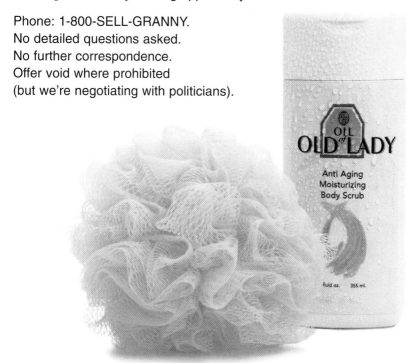

We've discovered the secret to youthful-looking skin
...and what to do about granny ®

Where toilet water really

France's *Eau de toilette* region still a mystery to most.

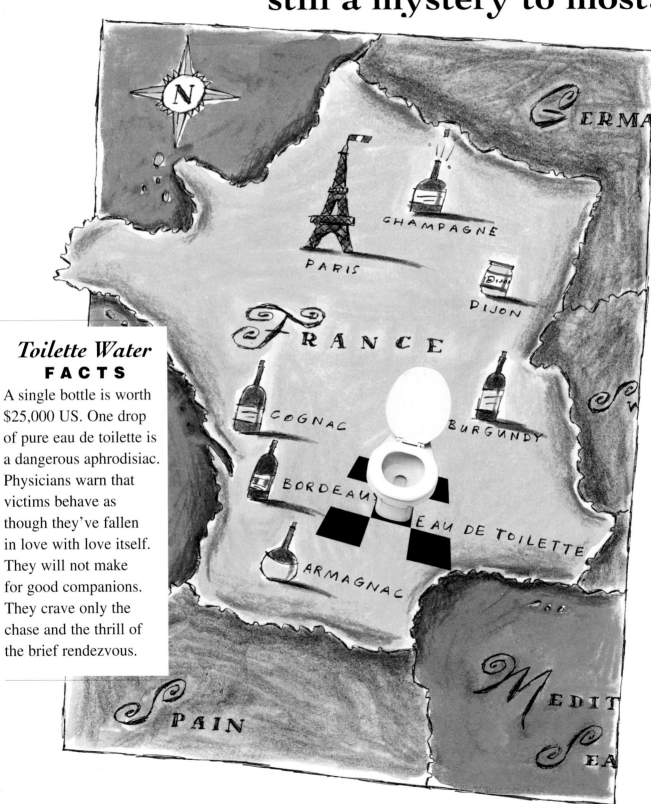

Toilette Water
FACTS

A single bottle is worth $25,000 US. One drop of pure eau de toilette is a dangerous aphrodisiac. Physicians warn that victims behave as though they've fallen in love with love itself. They will not make for good companions. They crave only the chase and the thrill of the brief rendezvous.

comes from.

Perhaps you consider yourself a connoisseur of the finer things in life? Can you *hold your own* against the best? VAGUE bets that when it comes to the origin of toilet water, even the most cultured individual will discover they're still a little wet behind the ears.

There is a place in France where the water trickles forth by its own free will, appears out of practically nowhere with only a little help from humans. Hand ladled with great care by peasant workers who know why they're there. They are not in any great rush; they can't be. They must wait and be patient with the understanding that you cannot prod the will of nature with the same stick that you discipline the obstinate swine. The region of which I speak is known to those of good breeding as *EAU DE TOILETTE*

Close to some of the most famous wine regions in the world there is a region unlike any other, where a very special industry quietly *goes* about its *business* practically unnoticed. Yet each year they do more than a billion dollars' worth of business in a world market which they alone dominate.

When it comes to the originality of liquids the French are fiercely territorial. If you produce bubbly you better not call it champagne unless it actually comes from the region of Champagne. So why would one expect it to be any different when it comes to toilet water? If it doesn't say eau de toilette on the label, it may not even come from toilets, and it definitely doesn't come from the region of Eau de toilette.

Long before Jean-Luc de Bastarde popularized toilet water, the custom of putting something

"If it doesn't say Eau de toilette on the label, it doesn't come from toilets."

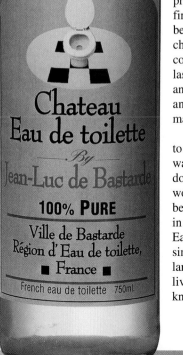

sweet-smelling behind the ears was introduced by the French. Since that time it has become almost as popular as the annoying practice of double mock kissing on both sides of the face (Mmmwha! Mmmwha! Mmmwha! Mmmwha!).

"Wine maketh glad zee heart of man, but zee toilet wataire, she is seemply grande."

—Jean-Luc de Bastarde

Both are examples of "Pretense de la France" and have spread throughout the civilized world.

Pure toilet water is older than the toilet itself. Gathered from the bowl at the peak of perfection, it's trod on by tender loving feet to enhance and release precious character traits. Then it's immediately plunged into wooden casks so that the air cannot get at it, and aged in oxygen-free storage for two years.

When the waiting is over, the casks are brought out into the sunlight for the filtering off of the salty sediment. It is a special day, a celebration of the bounty of the bowl. The priest is presented with the first bottle, and after it has been blessed the bell in the church steeple rings and continues to do so until the last bottle has been corked and sealed with a washer and lock-nut. Everyone marvels at the clarity.

At long last, it is ready to be shipped to the toilet water manufacturers. The doings are done but the work is not over. It must begin again as it always has in the tiny region known as Eau de toilette. They are a simple people with a singular purpose, living out their lives the only way they know how.

Château
Eau de toilette
By
Jean-Luc de Bastarde
100% PURE
Ville de Bastarde
Région d'Eau de toilette,
■ France ■
French eau de toilette 750ml.

New Minimal Terry Towel Body Wra
available in 12 exciting colors ($675
Terry Towel Head Wrap ($325)
available at Yaks Fifth Avenue

FROM
KARL
It's the

I DON'T HAVE A THING TO WEAR!

FRESH FROM THE SHOWER
COLLECTION

Oh yes you do.
What could be simpler?
You emerge from the
shower and while
still dripping wet
wrap yourself in a towel
and off you go to the
airport onto a private jet,
destination unknown.
It's free, bold, radical,
fluffy, absorbent,
unconventional styling
—it's the least you can do.

new minimalism
LAGERHEAD
east you can do

The Divine House of Krishna Dior

Remember us? We used to annoy you in airports!

Harry Krishna, CEO and head designer, is wearing Krishna Dior's
i AM NOT THIS SHIRT t-shirt ($90)
Saffron-orange pants ($120)
Kama Sutra jacket ($650)
sports sunglasses ($85)
designer forehead dot ($8.50)

In the beginning, God created *Christian Dior.* Then, out of the blue another religion picked up on the successful Dior name and built an empire based on one simple question, "Do you have any spare change?"

Times have changed since the early days, and Krishna Dior's marketing focus is no longer restricted to hitting up the traveling public for loose change before they board a jetliner. In fact, Krishna execs now board airliners of their own as they run a door-to-door network that matches those of Avon and Mary Kay. In addition, they own and operate legitimate boutiques in airports, shopping malls and upscale chain stores worldwide.

Financial experts scratch their heads, wondering how a bunch of passive street corner panhandlers ended up with a five hundred million dollar empire without involving backers or incurring a bank loan. Such skepticism amuses company CEO and head designer Harry Krishna.

"The answer is simple," he says with a smile. "We may look funny, but we understand an important aspect of human behavior. We observed that, first, if you are annoying, people will tell you to go away. Second, if you are annoying *enough,* people will *pay* you to go away. We based our business plan on the second scenario."

Ramma Ramma Ding Dong Move Over Avon Here Comes Krishna Dior

Krishna Dior embarked on a business venture which created a new fashion giant. The company's first initiative was to develop Dior to Door® sales. The approach went like so: Polite sales people wearing orange pants arrive at the door with their merchandise. The occupant of the home is presented with an attractive catalog. While the customer browses, the salesperson showers them with love, does a little dance, chants a few songs and writes up the order—all in a low pressure environment. Three days later they return with the goods and the transaction is complete. True, it's a bit of a song and dance routine, but the experience is so weird that people are falling in love with the saffron disciples of divine design.

It's a far cry from asking for handouts on street corners in exchange for that massive impossible-to-comprehend volume on eastern religion (which does, by the way, make for a delightful doorstop).

> **"If you are reincarnated as *Bullwinkle the Moose*—and obviously you're not a size 8 anymore—Krishna Dior's GUARANTEED FOR LIFE AFTER LIFE REFUND POLICY allows you to return the outfit any time in the future—no questions asked. This makes Krishna Dior the first design house in fashion history to not only stand behind their products but in front of them as well."**

The Karma Lottery®

But, the most unusual aspect of Krishna Dior's sales strategy is surely the Karma Lottery Scratch 'n' Win ticket—one comes free with every purchase. Those lucky enough to hold a winning ticket receive *Good Karma Points* —anywhere from 10 (don't laugh—it's the difference between coming back as a squid or a dog) to 40,000 (which guarantees demigod status after death, along with dinner for two at the Krishna Curry Palace).

Says Harry Krishna: "Everyone is willing to pack reincarnation away somewhere in the back of their mind. It's unnerving enough concentrating on *this* life without worrying about what you may be faced with in the next as a result of shortsightedness. How many little people—or even cockroaches—are we safely allowed to squash in this life without seriously inconveniencing ourselves on the next plane of existence through bad karma? Will I be moving forward or back? Should I invest in stocks or treasury bills? These are the questions we must all ask ourselves."

Such disarming honesty is typical of the man—and he has made sure it is reflected in his company's sales policy.

"When people are out shopping, store employees will tell them that an outfit is *becoming* just so the salesperson can make the sale... 'Oh, it's YOU! It's definitely YOU!' I do not believe in this approach. It's not what's on the outside that counts. Clothes do not really *become* you unless one is inclined not to do laundry; then you have a problem."

His styles are about reliability and overall comfort. They assault and confuse the eye, brilliantly breaking every rule in the book. "My designer t-shirts are printed with the words 'I am not this shirt,'" says Krishna. It is a subtle reminder that the clothes do not make the man or the woman.

Is Krishna saying that clothes are merely useless outer layers? He nods. "Clothes are only essential in that we, in the civilized world, are required to wear them by law. In the larger picture nothing is essential except knowledge through a spiritual existence. We teach our customers that the clothes we sell are, in reality, illusions, practically worthless. We also point out that the wads of cash they hold are also worthless. So why not swap a worthless $2,500 for our worthless attractive silk robe with matching accessories?"

But nowhere is Krishna Dior's integrity more evident than in their approach to sex. "Most of our competitors use sex to sell. They spout off slogans like, "Buy our stuff and get laid." This is an empty promise. I prefer to concentrate on our one simple promise: 'Guaranteed for life... after life... after life...' Our clothes follow you to the next level of existence. If you are reincarnated as Bullwinkle the Moose and the outfit doesn't fit anymore— we'll give you your money back. Although, quite frankly, if you spring for our top-of-the-line Kama Sutra Suit you'll be like heaven to touch—more likely to come back as a mink. Then you'll get laid far more than the Armani set!"

With increased popularity in New Age and the mass exodus away from traditional organized religions, the public seems to be very receptive to Krishna Dior's spiritual and fashion consciousness pitch.

Once again, for whatever reason, the Hare Krishna have not only attracted attention but have managed to secure an enthusiastic following. Is it the haircuts, their fashion line, the mystifying chants or a transcendental combination of all three? This is a question for the fashion historians to argue about. But if history teaches us one thing, it is this: If you dress funny, sing annoyingly loud, love thy neighbor as thyself and, most importantly, ask for the sale, you will attract enough followers and customers to make the cash register ring.

Krishna Dior's **Blue Mood Love Oil** ($69) available at Yaks Fifth Avenue or Dior to Door.

> **"The amazing success of Krishna Dior is really something to chant about."**

Krishna Dior's **Tri-Eye sunglasses** because the third eye needs protection too! ($135)

Attention Valued Readers!

BUSINESS REPLY MAIL
FIRST-CLASS MAIL   PERMIT NO 666   BOULDER CO

POSTAGE WILL BE PAID BY ADDRESSEE

VAGUE

**PO BOX 36-25-36
BOULDER COLORADO**

NO POSTAGE
NECESSARY
IF MAILED
IN THE
UNITED STATES

We've nailed this annoying little subscription card onto the page so you won't bang your head on the coffee table while attempting to pick it up after it bounces off your crotch and happily flutters to the floor. Why are we being so nice to you? Well, it occurred to us that if you really wanted to frost our socks you could cause us a great deal of sorrow and financial strife. It costs us about 25 cents every time one of these subscription forms is returned to us—that really adds up. However, when people take a subscription to Vague we work the cost of processing into the price. But if everybody picked the business reply card up off the floor, marched it over to a mail box and dropped it in without filling out the handy address form on the back, we would end up getting charged for it. Now, we don't want to put any brainy ideas in your head, but here is the worst-case scenario. Every month one million annoying little cards are dropped into the mail box without a return address on them—we end up paying for

all of them without getting a lousy subscription out of it. Each month it costs us $250,000. Multiply that figure by twelve and over the course of a year we would lose $3 million. Our knees start to quiver and we're now shaking in our Gucchie booties. Now, multiply $3 million times three years and we have a full-scale epidemic on our hands. Perhaps even the end of fashion as we know it. So you can see why a few nails from the local hardware store are a small investment compared to what could happen if we didn't feel you were such a lovely group of body perfect women whom we love dearly. We can't begin to tell you what your responsible behavior and patronage mean to us. In fact, we wouldn't call you overweight and unattractive—even if you were. Besides, what does a little on the hefty side and not too pleasing to look at have to do with anything? So, if you follow the advice laid out in our editorial and buy all of the products advertised by our corporate sponsors, you could actually start enjoying a quality of life normally reserved for the "supermodels."

KRISHNA DIOR

when orange pants ruled the west

UMBERTO GARBA

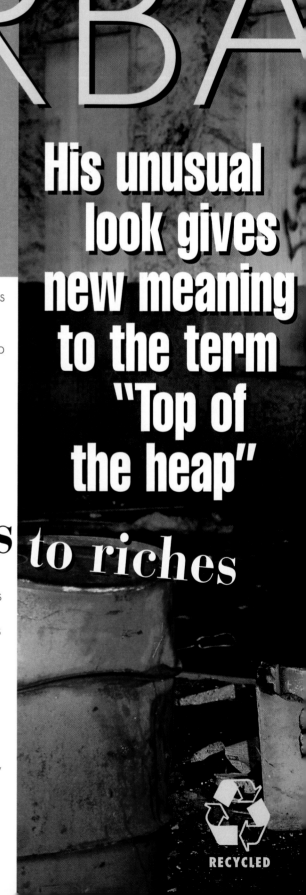

THE DESIGNER WHO'S TURNING TRASH INTO CASH

When corporate downsizing came into business fashion it created a new niche in the fashion market place. This season Umberto Garbaggio's wardrobe downsize without compromise has helped ease the pain of the recession and is exciting news for the "Nouveau Impoverished."

With the celebrated release of his fabulous recycled materials collection, Umberto Garbaggio has reintroduced the "bag lady." His inspired designs are sure to stop traffic as well as cater to the budgets of the once affluent but recently fired. As waste disposal and recycling issues become more upfront and personal in our daily lives, his unusual look will give new meaning to the term "Top of the Heap."

His unusual look gives new meaning to the term "Top of the heap"

from bags to riches

"I insist on using only the finest rubbish. I wouldn't dream of scouring public dumps for cheaper waste materials and my clients can rest assured that items such as recycled colostomy bags are a definite no-no. They will never—even accidentally—find their way into my collections. I negotiate with reliable suppliers who pay special attention to each design detail—each specific requirement. I salvage and give old materials a rich, exciting, glamorous new look. Today's designers must be as resourceful as the customers they serve. Women who wear my collections are thrilled to discover they can still achieve the look of *rich-bitch* for thousands less."

RECYCLED

GGIO

Vague photographer Stanislav Switalski surprises supermodels
Nikki Tyler and Woo Paul on a dash-for-the-trash shopping spree
at fashionable *Cul-de-Saks* on New York's Avenue E.

UMBERTO GARB

RECYCLED

Sleeveless in Seattle

This season the sleeves are gone, celebrating America's constitutional right to "bare arms."

Nikki Tyler in sleeveless orange garbage bag evening dress with flower appliqué ($850)